The Finger Bone

. . . .

Books by Kevin Prufer

Strange Wood
The Finger Bone
Fallen from a Chariot
National Anthem
In a Beautiful Country
Churches

Edited Volumes

New Young American Poets
Dark Horses: Poets on Overlooked Poems (with Joy Katz)
New European Poets (with Wayne Miller)
Dunstan Thompson: On the Life & Work of a Lost American Master (with D. A. Powell)
Until Everything is Continuous Again: Essays on the Work of W. S. Merwin
(with Jonathan Weinert)
Russell Atkins: On the Life & Work of an American Master (with Michael Dumanis)

THE FINGER BONE

Kevin Prufer

CARNEGIE MELLON UNIVERSITY PRESS
Pittsburgh 2013

ACKNOWLEDGMENTS

ACM: "Writing the Accident" as "On Writing Well"; *The Antioch Review*: "Women and Maple Tree"; *Boulevard*: "Pause, Pause," "Outdoor Café, Approaching Storm"; *Chelsea*: "The Wreckers"; *Cimarron Review*: "Lab Nightmare," "Pastoral," Things are Inherent in Things"; *Connecticut Review*: "Astronomer's Prayer," "Neanderthal"; *Electronic Poetry Review*: "Helicopter Wreck," What is this ship?"; *Flint Hills Review*: "Death Comes in the Form of a Pontiac Trans Am," "Moth Knowledge"; *Flyway*: "Infant Nephew"; *Fourteen Hills*: "The Living"; *Green Mountains Review*: "The End of the City"; *Hayden's Ferry Review*: "Letter of Consolation"; *The Laurel Review*: "Ars Poetica," "For the Dead: Adoration"; *LIT*: "The Lastof the Storm Windows," "The Astronomer to His Telescope"; *The Literary Review*: "Sensual Disaster"; *Meridian*: "This was the model to which I held"; *New Letters*: "Salvage Lot, Dusk," "From the Auto Wreck"; *Mid-American Review*: "For the Unfortunates"; *Notre Dame Review*: "Trompe L'Oeil," "Petals," "For the Dead," ("Are you smooth as the curve"), "For the Dead," ("A gray wind gutters the fireflies"), "For the Dead: Adoration," and "For the Dead," ("The fact that I still imagine"); *Phoebe*: "The Archaeologist's Evening Prayer"; *Ploughshares*: "Blue Pitcher, Empty and Full"; *Prairie Schooner*: "Divorce," "Spin Out"; *Quarterly West*: "Report from the Lovelorn," Adolescence"; *Rhizome*: "Nancy Drew and the Secret"; *River City*: "The Lucky Criminals," "My Other Self," "A Man in Pearls"; *River Styx*: "The Astronomer's Dream," as "Mad Scientist," "Overheard in a Restaurant"; *Shenandoah*: "Narcissism"; *The Southern Review*: "Sad Song," "The Boys," "Terrible Love"; *Southwest Review*, "Sad Story"; *Sycamore Review*, "Kinds of Sleep," "Stars Where They Aren't"; *TriQuarterly*: "Frightened Figure with Horse"; *Western Humanities Review*: "Two Muses Discuss Arrowheads"; *Willow Springs*: "The God of Clues"; *Witness*: "What the Paymaster Said," "Technophobic Sonnet."

"Kinds of Sleep" was reprinted in *The Pushcart Prize Anthology XXVI*, 2002. "Divorce and "Spin-Out" received the 2001 Strousse/Prairie Schooner Award. "Sad Story" was reprinted in *American Diaspora, Poetry of Exile*, published by the University of Iowa Press, 2001. "Kinds of Sleep" was reprinted in *9mm, Poets Respond to Violence in America*, University of Iowa Press, 2001. "Two Muses Discuss Arrowheads" was reprinted in *I Have My Own Song For It*, University of Akron Press, 2002. "What the Paymaster Said" was reprinted in *Clockpunchers: Poems of the American Workplace*, Partisan Press, 2001. "Nancy Drew and the Secret" was reprinted in *PMPA*, the publication of the Missouri Philological Association. Thanks to Walter Bargen, Mary Hallab, Joy Katz, Rose Marie Kinder, Susan Ludvigson, Susan Steinberg, Ann Townsend, and Sharon Wahl for their valuable insight and criticism.

The Finger Bone was first published in 2002
by Carnegie Mellon University Press.

First Classic Contemporaries Edition, April 2013

Library of Congress Control Number: 2012949878
ISBN: 978-0-88748-570-1

Cynthia & John

One

. . . .

PASTORAL

This is the season when wasps come back.
The yellow ones, many-chambered and implausible,
have thawed from the downed limbs where they slept their last,
have dug their way out of the six-inch holes.

It is the season of the divided-in-parts,
the worm with the eleven-sectioned heart
that beats in its parcels as the pink ends twitch.
It is the season of egg sacks from the traffic lights

that fall to the road when they thin and burst.
There are rows of angels on the power lines
like crows or snarls where the sun comes up.
Are they warm or unmasked as the volts run through?

Are they damp in the sun's surpassing glow?
They are crying because they don't know what to do with us.
Their wings flex a thousand times a second.
They say *beautiful, beautiful,* and peer through our windows.

Come out where the yard is complex and awake.
Strange as a birth from a wormwood hole—
like wasps, they're a tension of nervous wings.
Like rainstorms, they'll weep us into spring.

ADOLESCENCE

The little sleep in the melon, the seeds
swaying on strings in the hollow of it,

rolled from a brown bag onto the counter.
The overripe doze, the dream

beneath its skin: the sun. And not just that,
but the meat, the possibility

of light and glisten. Softening,

and sweet, the melon at rest
like a boy's dreaming head, like a shelter,

a house that is not a ruin yet, but will be

someday, or a boy asleep on the sofa,
the boy dreaming that now,

now the roof's caved in. Now the termites
are in the woodwork, now the house

is a shudder on stilts, now the water
is rolling, is rotting them away.

The melon, asleep as it always is,
the house crumbling to its knees on the beach

and the boy awash inside, knowing
some time, soon, yes,

knowing the light will find him here,
in the clasp of it, the cup

of the palms of his hands that open,

unstoppably, like a melon opens,
into a second age.

SAD STORY

The waves are not part of us. What sand they touch and overskim, —
the seaglass flecks—once part of us, no longer,

in the slow grind of their curving away. They are cats' eyes on the verge
of closing, eyes in the sand. I am too far away from home.

————————————

A slat fell out of the dock and drifted toward the shore—boardslip
and groan. The waves are impersonal as math. If I could slide into them

I would not know what to say to myself. I think my hair
would twist around my neck. My words always embarrass me

————————————

before the enormous. I want a second chance—east and homeward.
This sand is a handful of forgetting, an eyeful of pain. Blooddrop of pain.

WHAT IS THIS SHIP?

What is this sleep? The waves lull me to it.
Heavy body, whimper in a curl of surf—

What is this wave but a rocking in my sleep?
Slip of sea where a far ship's fires reflect.

Sleep, sleep—sometimes I am almost dead,
floating like a tired raft in a slow tide.

Or I am an unknotted raft whose boards
are soft where a leak seeps in.

Guilt, guilt a distant foremast says
in its creak and gutter

while a dull wind shudders past the sails,
pushes them out like breath.

It would be better if he were cast into the sea
a cross about his neck. It would be better—

In a dream I was cast into a sea
while the men on the deck

put their hands to their mouths
and cried. I lay on my back

and the men said, *Sin,* their voices woody
and sad. The hope was I would find a cure

for the push of waves that wetted my boards.
But the sky was a rope stretched over the surf,

my body turning like a raft at sea.

TERRIBLE LOVE

Wish the lights would go back on, wish it was spring already.
Wish the bees would fly back home from my living room.
Hear them singing and horsing around in there? Rattle, rattle
against the porcelain, fire screen, window panes, their unfeeble buzz
rising to racket-level til one by one the portraits fall from the walls.
They enjoy the glow the space heater provides.

When we moved in here—my young wife and I—the place was merely
tumble-down: chips in the walls, blackened floors, and leaves spreading,
        fan-like,
from the cracks beneath the doors. We unloaded the bed first.
I said, "we'll consummate things here—and here, and here," pointing
first to that bed, and then to the leafswept places. She stood in the kitchen
unloading the flatware. One by one, her forks tumbled to the floor.

I was terribly in love, but it wasn't long
before she shuddered at my breath on her neck. She is a woman
of great distractions and hairpins. I swept the leaves from the doorways
and her laughs came as blackish clouds, her words snowdots or beetles,
        depending.
Sometimes I wouldn't see her all day, so busy was she
singing to herself in the gardens behind the house. I swept and swept,
cleaned the pipes, caulked the walls as best I could.

Then it was November and the ice thickened
in invisible leaks in the bricks. When the winds came, the trees shook
their twig-tips until the windows cracked. The bees arrived later,
sensing, somehow, the house an escape from the cold.
Wish they were gone. Wish I had something to clot the walls.
My wife, in her bedrobe, drew an invisible line
at the foot of the stairs. "Here is for you," she told me, sweeping
the downstairs with her hand. Now she lives in the master chamber
at the top of the stairs. All day, behind the bees, I hear
ice cracking in those leaky veins. The bricks fall, startlingly,
into the yard. Sometimes I hear her slippers skipping over my head.
She sings to herself and moves the bed around. Is she tying
a great escape from the bed sheets? Does she scale
the rose trellises at night? And for whom? My poor skin

is brailled over with stings. I wish the spring storms would come.
Wish the gardens would bloom, thorn over the path to the road.
Wish there was something I could say.

REPORT FROM THE LOVELORN

When the light goes down on Kansas,
the endless field of rustling corn
becomes the flat of a black moth's wing.
It quivers in the starlight, flexes,

flexes. And an old man sits on the porch
opposite mine. When he inhales,
the tip of his cigarette glows like a distant headlight.
There is nothing here but corn, the granary, a few old houses,

all of us living on the shivering surface of a black wing.
You might almost say the passing trucks are insane,
tilting toward the wing's edge, hissing like the committed
at the bottoms of their tires.

THE LUCKY CRIMINALS

We are not equal to our criminals. A raftful floats by every day,
dainty blue canopies flaring in the breeze. Cigarettes dangling

from downturned mouths, eyes screwed to the shore—
the criminals are slim and beautiful, draped

in their lawnchairs so their fingers leave trails in the river water.
They are sentimental and lean, shirtless and droop-eyed.

Oh to dig my tired toes into the soft mud of the bank,
the pickpocket says. *To drop coins in the river and retrieve them,*

to retrieve all the coins that have ever been dropped in the river.
The others are silent, smoke leaking from their mouths. Wishes

are everything to criminals, and the burl of black clouds over the trees
is unimportant. *My father was buried with a mouthful*

of stolen gems, the con-man replies, swiping his guitar. *I dug*
one hundred holes in the yard before I found them. The black clouds

curl into mouths that rustle the trees. Around their feet,
fifteen bags of coins. The hacker picks his golden teeth, the falsely accused

stares hungrily to our shore. Our women are in love with criminals.
They have the soft glow of lamplight on pavement on clear nights after rain.

How we envy criminal ambition. We are strung like pearls
on the weedy shore, white-faced and furious as they pass.

Our dinner burns, our children cry, and the wind cools
as the storm sweep over. *Justice, justice*, we call to them.

But the long-fingered criminals in their gorgeous swimsuits,
the lawless with their guns draped over their chairs, the shifty-eyed

and doomed with bare chests, the exciting—they'll never notice us.

Infant Nephew

My zero, my thumbtack,
stone in my shoe, you

of no memory at all,
too easily growled to bed

by tires cutting the rain-slick street.
You, whose mind sleeps

in the porch light, all hunger
and thumbs, swiveling low

into my unsteady arms.
I don't know how to deal

with the perfect, the at peace,
the easily bruised

and asleep. The grass-tips
curve and the storm clouds blink

for you. *Sleep, sleep now,*
I am singing.

My bit of chalk, my wrinkle,
my oblivious.

PAINTED CUP

I gave my father a painted cup
which he turned in his brittle hands.

The glare of the lamp on its porcelain, dull shadow
at the bottom—cup with painted sea reeds

and a starry night, cup of breath, of air.
Cup with a handle like a heron's neck.

He brushed his fingers over the curved rim.
He touched its lip, the skirt at the base.

———————————

Sometimes I am a scratch on such a cup.
But leave it on the front porch on a windy day,

the palms will pour their fronds into it.
Put it in the freezer and glaze it with frost,

bury it in the sand where the beach begins—
For a sip of the water that could fill it,

salt water warmed where the sea rifts part and glow,
warmed where the blind fish spread their gills.

DIVORCE

All of the names have been changed
Someone had entered the yard that night

In order to protect the innocent,
My mother, we'll call her Cynthia,

Was in the kitchen watering the plants
That decorated the country house windows

When suddenly she heard a sawing from the woods,
This is a true story,

Out back behind the house
When a strange man

Cut the largest tree with a crash into the moss
And such a cloud of dust and birds

Rose to the treetops and beyond

*

Mine was the wisp of hair that came lovingly to her cheek
Mine was the breath against the silk of the blouse

But whose was the saw that leveled the tree,
And the second tree? One by one,

The trees fell, and this, a true story,
Though the names have been changed,

The two of us afraid, in a way,
In the dark, even to open

The front door and call into the black woods,
Though I, only a child, we'll call me

By my own name,
And she, Cynthia, tangled in all this

Watering can in hand, paused
Over the spider plant and the dishes not even done,

The Jeep parked on the gravel drive,
Not a telephone between there and town,

And my father—we'll call him that—
Who knew what he was thinking

At that very moment   What could we do?   So
To protect the innocent

We turned off the house lights one by one
Locked the doors as, at that very moment,

A laughing from the woods just outside the house

*

Difficult to describe, though it sounded not unlike
The sound of the saw if I must make it clear

Up, up into the attic we crawled
And out with those lights, too, until

In retrospect, in the darkness,
There were so many things that horrible year:

The bursting of dams, my brother also gone, the letters
Always laughing in the mailbox, and forever somewhere

Someone, anonymous, hungry
Mine was the crying into Cynthia's skirt,

Mine was, finally, the lost-in-sleep
In the air beneath the attic window,

With the nameless man in the yard,
That, by sunup, was scattered with the black half-fingers

Of this, the strange true story, the remains of our trees.

NANCY DREW AND THE SECRET

"Mystery or no mystery," the woman said,
"the family must eat."
Nancy, her blond hair still damp from the swim,
skipped lightly up the carpeted stairway
and tiptoed into her father's den.

Tall, handsome Carson Drew
thrust his hands into his pockets.
Nancy thought she saw something moving.
"Come on, Dad," she said,
"let me in on the mystery."

All the windows were dark.
Nancy thought she saw something moving
in the rhododendrons next to the porch steps.
That was odd, she thought.
"Hello!" Nancy cried. "Hello!"

She was halfway up the walk.
Someone whirled her around
and forced her toward the convertible.
The arm was tight against Nancy's throat,
a man's arm in a rough coat sleeve.

His thumb pressed unbearably.
Somehow she must give an alarm!
She tried to scream, but her voice
was weak and small. His thumb pressed
unbearably. *The horn!*

She leaned on it with all her weight.
Presently, Mr. Beaman's front door
flew open. A voice bellowed:
"Say, you look pretty shaky, Nancy.
Sure you're all right?"

Nancy thought she saw something moving.
"Mystery or no mystery," the woman said,
"the family must eat"

"Come on, Dad," she said.
"Let me in on the mystery."

Two

. . . .

THE WRECKERS

Conch-eared and dirty, slick in our jeans—we had a stylish
consumption,
               an elegant crook in each bony arm, the long lashes
of girls. Elbow to elbow—we rode the smooth seats of stolen cars,
threw bottles out the window and into the sea.
                            The Wreckers and I
were morose in black leather and white faces, dangerous, a studded
dog collar around each pale neck. Bad, bad we said
                                 under our breath
pressed thigh-to-thigh, laughing until the windows fogged
and the streetlights winked like drops at the tips of a hundred syringes.

And when a cloud scuttled down like a great moth's wing
and darkened the street,
                     we'd pull to the curb and scratch our names
into the new paint jobs of sleeping cars. Gorgeous, the moon,
when it reappeared
               and the Wreckers and I laughed and laughed,
collapsed on the street corner next to the bums and the trash
and the silent alleys, coughing pills and cigarettes. We were that happy,

and that gone. Lord, where are my beautiful Wreckers now?
The city has slipped to the pavement like all the red leaves, it has fallen
and I cannot put it together.
                   And I've grown lazy and fat
so my jacket won't fit, so I do not think I'm beautiful any more.
I need to be up at seven, and washed. Boys, boys—
                         your streets are quiet
and your people are sleeping, so do something, come to my window
and wake me up with rocks. Do anything—terrific in your acid-wash,
in your buckles and hair glitter,
                   you were so perfect and pale,
like lingerie or new chalk. My slips of sad paper, my noisy wraiths—
we're all such awful wrecks now.

SPIN-OUT

The cue ball bounces out the bar door into the snow.
On the curb, beside their pickup, two boys throw bottle caps
at the wheels—*Goddamn,* one says, *the truck spun twice
on this ice sheet, bashed nose-first into the ditch*

*at the side of route BB. Got this cut on my head because of it,
see?* The face is small, yellow bangs snipped straight above the eyes,
but, when brushed aside, a red cut like a smile right there,
just below the hairline. Because the day's already gone,

the other leans forward to look close: gloom and warm breath
on the injured face. The truck radio exchanges country songs.
*Had my head right there, in the steering wheel,
was out, gone, cold, tipped clear forward in this ditch.*

Could've froze like that. Another bottle cap tossed and rattling
across the street, a stranger cursing the missing ball,
the uninjured examining, now, the crumpled fender. *I tell you,
I tell you,* and a shaking of the blond head. A tapping

of pool sticks behind the door, two puffs from the boys' mouths.
Dusk falls like God's own black breath. *Close one,
close one*—the fingers trace the scar. Everywhere, cars slide
into guardrails, veer over snowy berms. Like ice in the eye of God,

a street lamp glitters from the crease in the pickup's fender.

SALVAGE LOT, DUSK

The cars are very sleepy, the cars are soft
in their rivets and rotted joints. All evening,

the sun oranged and grew. All evening—
a blotting out of trees, a towering of hulls,

each axle like a thief's chopped arm.
And which trunk holds the body? In every trunk,

with a busted tire or sprung umbrella.
In every car, hands roped at her waist,

cheek to the floor, eyes rolled up or away,
knifed in the back. The junkyard's a silence

and the girl won't wake. The sun falls
like a body, engorged, in love

with itself. And out on Route 50, the traffic
slows, a red line of brake lights, an artery

stopped. The gorgeous, ordinary glow
of the neon sign, the dull light on the face

of the boy who sits beneath it, eating grapes,
waiting for a ride that never comes—

to him, the world's a quiver, a little song
in an empty room. *I should get up*, he thinks,

I should shout or fire a gun in the air.
A thin moon slips over the cars,

an airplane drones the lot away.

SENSUAL DISASTER

This is about the strength of the airplane's hull,
the red bloom of tail lights, the milk of wings

cutting vapor into smiles. Unknown to the wasp
or the radio needle, we shift in our joints when the winds

breathe over, adjust to the stir of the cockpit's
purr. We work crosswords or doze into chairs.

Who wouldn't choose to die this way, without warning?—
if, silently, the airplane should open like a toy.

And what would we see? The pause, infinitesimal,
as wind ruffles the hair of the others, suspended

in slumber, white arms draped loosely into the aisles?
Or those at the windows, fingers to the scratched panes?

What will our thoughts be, as the seatbelts tighten to our husks
and the metal groans at its rivets?

How will we be strewn, when this is over?

HELICOPTER WRECK

See the long islands—ochre, cliff-rippled, wrinkled as scabs, their pine tips
scratching the pink sky? No motor boats today. The bay sinks
into its silence. Mine is the drowned head,

                                   restored. Mine, the tilted-
to-the-low-sun eyes, the gaping, the outstretched, fingers rippling
over, thin skin loosening where the nails begin. I list; my boots

lag behind, or below, currents depending. What can I say, my teeth
salted over, the last of the sun cataracting my eyes? Far below,
the wreck of the helicopter lolls:

                              lopped rotors, glass bubble caved in,
        seatbelts shot
and empty now, flapping. My old sunglasses rock in the wet sand with
        the shards.
Either I am an uneventful thing, or I am graceful, or both,

by which I mean I might be sleeping. First I felt a sputter, a lurch,
half audible. Then, the rotors skipped, cracked, and fell past the windows
into the bay. The cockpit filled with smoke,

                               sweet smoke, as plastic
        or cinnamon
to the burner is sweet. Then the windows wetted over. I unclipped
the seatbelts, the whole earth tipped. It's been days and hours now.

My new eyes startle me: The black birds lift, one by one, from the tree tops.
See the feathery tufts, the beaks half-gaped, bellies tight, talons tip-to-tip?

Where the bay throws dead fish into the cliff ridges, the flies twirl—
        in each eye
a refracted arc, the black on blue, where water meets air—
        my uptilted head.

WRITING THE ACCIDENT

The hands remain calm, only the fingers move. It is the art of the gorilla.
Or it is the art of the disembodied head, the computer diskette,
        the breeze

rustling the grass tips. Say the life-lift helicopter
goes down on the corner of Pine and 22nd, its rotors chirping up sparks

from the pavement, its glass bubble collapsing into cracks.
Some are beating on horns, closing eyes, touching brake pedals.

Others stand in a thickening ring as the power lines twist
once more into the propeller and the fire truck pulls sleepily forward.
        Everyone

waits for some motion from the cockpit, or, otherwise, a sudden bursting
into flame. Here is art for calm hands, for an empty space in an overcast
        sky.

Here is something for the innocent glass to swallow. Otherwise, a crow
flaps to a stop on the nearest telephone pole, looks the other way.
        Is he uncaring?

Burned-out wick, dusk through a hole in the wall, a black seed?
Like a deranged thought, he flexes his wing tips, lowers his neck,
        beak stretched

to a low sound—there is nothing here for an empty stomach.
Once, twice—while the rotors catch on the pavement and the crowd ahs,

while the rest of us lumber dully in the street,
while the grass yellows and the memory, days later, hums
        in the disk drive—

once, twice, the black wings—and he lifts into the sky.

Things are Inherent in Things

The Hotel Paradiso was on fire.
The red trucks pulled up, their crystal sirens singing,
then, one by one, the guests threw themselves from the windows
into the wide eyes the firemen unfolded.

I parted the curtains. Far below, the Italians
had gathered in the streets, gape-mouthed, yellow-faced.
I watched a man land on the sweet spot, bounce once,
then roll on his side coughing smoke.
Another, a young woman, just to the left of my window, clung to the sill,
arms stretched taught, burning skirt in the updraft
like an enormous yellow flower.

My own door warmed over.
The crack below it spit smoke. It wasn't long before the room smelled
of tar, hot plastic, sulfur, and, strangely, cinnamon.
I could not bring myself to peer through the glass hole
into the hall. Neither could I wave or shout my presence
to those below, but sat by the window on the edge of the bed,
a towel around my waist, wet from the shower
until the lights went out.

One thing, I believe, is inherent in another—shadows in clouds,
laughter in the mouth, smoke or flames in what is combustible.
Have I been awful in my life?
I have friends. I call my mother each week long-distance,
am good to those I work with—even generous.
The contracts, spread across the bed, could burn. The briefcase could burn,
and so could each diskette. I would not trade them for myself

or another, but watched the paramedics far below
swab twenty guilty breathing bodies
as the crowd gasped and stared. Like an inhuman eye,
a red light blinked as the ambulances pulled away.
We are deranged, I thought, building our rooms so high.
Deranged—the hotel roof coughing fire, the windows choking on their own glass.
And the people in the street, faces lit, eyes dilated,
in each pupil a single orange spark—also, deranged.

PAUSE, PAUSE

Praise to the empty schoolroom, when the folders
are stowed and the sighing desktops close.

Praise to the sixteen-hour silence
after the last chairleg complains against the tiles.

There are tracks in the snow on the sidewalk,
ice salting into the bootprints. Snow clots fall

like good advice from the branches.
See the plaid skirts ticking into the distance?

The bookbags swaying to the footfalls?
Praise to the sun. It sets like a clocktower face,

oranges over, grows. Praise,
praise to the classrooms, empty at last.

One by one, the door-bolts click
and the lightbulbs shudder to a close.

The chairs dream all askew. Praise to the empty
hallway, the pause before the long bells cry.

OVERHEARD IN A RESTAURANT

The study of history is the best medicine for a sick mind. For instance,
there is an ancient city living in the dark
                                    on my tongue. When whatever God it is
opens my mouth and makes me speak, the city buzzes to life, foretelling
its own demise:
                    stones crumbling, events unfolding exactly, I tell you, as will be
recorded in the books years from now. Finally, what once hummed with
underground baths, vaults
                            secret as the insidious thoughts of the elected body,
will be buried, crushed inward, collapsed under its own misbegotten weight.
The other patrons at their tables
                            turn and stare, amused, aghast,
but, mostly, entertained. It is hard to keep my overfull mouth shut.

_____

Other times, I unclench my teeth, and everyone stops rattling
silver, stops stirring coffee spoons, and listens
                                    expecting a good story,
but what they get, finally, is the ticking of the clock on the ancient square,
the ignorant people,
                    each of them at their work behind one thousand windows,
blowing glass, stitching leather, filling out the countless forms, which are,
after all, necessary
                    to the goings-on of any city. History is, finally, a strange
and unpredictable thing. It turns on its heel and falls flat when you least expect it to,
but, mostly, it is uneventful.
                            This said, I have learned to keep my mouth closed,
the back of my tongue pressed firmly to my teeth.

_____

I might add that, beyond my tiny city, careful observation of your larger world
is essential to my stability.
                    See, over there, a cockroach balances
on the teacup's rim, contemplating, perhaps, the drop on either side.
The waiters constantly refill the water glasses.
                                    A man at the booth next to ours
leans over the table so his tie touches the edge of his plate and says, half seriously

to the woman whose long fingers curve around the stem of her glass,

                                                            If we miss
the play, there's always the couch and VCR at my place. Up to you.
She raises her eyebrows and smirks, but doesn't check her watch.

                                                    With my teeth
tight like this, the restaurant maintains its usual drone, that cigarette smell wafting
up and out of the smoking section, the ease and hiss of the front doors.

ARS POETICA

The bone in the ice cream, picked out, held
between the thumb and forefinger,

the startle of it, the catch in the breath,
the sick pit in the heart or stomach,

the queer blare of bone, of bloodspot
in the vanilla—the thought that this, perhaps,

is where something twittered away—
   ———

When it melts, ice cream is a thrill of rivulets,
is a sweet, pooling thing,

but the bone is blade-like
at the edges. Where did it come from?

Bird bone, finger bone, hollow as a flute
and playable, bleached and smooth to the thumb-

caress. The bone in the ice cream is terrible
   ———

and aches the teeth. How the face hurts
when the mouth bears down

on the cool, the strange, the gruesome truth
of it. What left the bone in the ice cream?

What cruel hand or wing, lopped and swirled away?
What bird? What angel? Splintered pointer,

flute that sings the sweetness away.

OUTDOOR CAFÉ, APPROACHING STORM

My mouth wants a handful of coins to fill it.
Somewhere, a car alarm sings to passersby.

The slamming of townhouse doors, the dip in the engine-whine
as a bus shifts gears, the thrum of airplanes over the city—

Sometimes, I have nothing to say. My tongue wets over
but my mouth is empty. A crow might pick a bit of foil

from the storm drain near a wheel rut. A crow
might simmer into the air—

———————————————

All travel ends in a glass city, a city
built as if of water. Like fishermen's nets,

the crows rise, a black grid,
each in their pink beaks—a glistening.

When I open the menu, too many wings
so the street hazes over with down. The wind always fails

to bring a storm. Everything has been said so well
I cannot do better.

Three

. . . .

TECHNOPHOBIC SONNET

Someone deleted the statues, I didn't know who.
All the stone men on horses were gone.
I had a mouthful of honey and nothing to speak to,
a gift in its wrapping, an empty lawn

where the park once was, where the statues stood.
They didn't up and walk away. They never moved.
But with a click in the snowfall, a hum from the woods
the men in carved boots, the horse on its hooves—

erased like a file from somebody's drive.
I wanted some answers—but the sky had that glow
of a computer's blue screen, the clouds like icons
that hovered too squarely. I wanted to know

where the statues went—when, with hardly a sound,
whoever it was shut his system down.

MOTH KNOWLEDGE

When suddenly the lights went out
I was counting the dustmoths at the observatory window.

Hundreds, wings like white hearts,
bodies pulsing invisibly.

I thought the light covered the wings
as powder. Once touched,

this also might coat the skin
and so, I thought, we whiten.

*

I heard a scratching from the yard,
a fluttering as if with one good wing

and one not so good.
But it was late, I couldn't see,

there were so many trees,
and the leaves so thick and black.

*

When the lights went out in the observatory,
the dustmoths swirled into the air

as so many stars. The screen
was metal, blackness, empty space

and the dim shapes of trees
coming slowly into focus

as my eyes sharpened
into the fine mesh.

*

The dead are perhaps as a telescope
aimed at what we at first presume

to be another receding star.
When we replace the lens covers

it is as if we closed an eye
and the information stopped.

THE ASTRONOMER TO HIS TELESCOPE

Weight the stars down. Tie them with threads
and tow them gently into the yard. Lash them
with strings. Tug them, as you would a kite
or a ship that has drifted too far into the bay.

Do you think them nonchalant? They love each word of praise.
They are already half in the water the rain has left.
Call them into their reflections. They won't singe us
or pervert your glass. They are too vain for that.

Like trees, they drizzle from gaudy leaves.
Like dryads, they strum the sky away.
Like sweet lounge singers, they turn our heads
all night. Applaud them down, before it's too late.

They are always thinking about the perfect exit—
redshift in the curve of your buffed glass eye.

THE ASTRONOMER'S PRAYER

—Charles Wright, *Zone Journals*

The lens fell out of the telescope.
The stars, by themselves, don't know a thing,

>> but constantly recede.

They ache in their redshift, they move quietly off
like a host at a party, drink-in-hand, introducing his guests
then stepping away.

> Pinwheel, lamp-glitter in the glass of wine—

the stars are inaccessible,

> touching their lips

to the snow where the grass pokes through, touching their lips
to the window panes.

> Without telescopes, we are thrice removed:

There are, first of all, the stars themselves, wrapped
in their recession. Then, our weak eyes, which cannot find them.

I think, also, we would look for them where they aren't,
which is our impulsive translation. The arc of the wineglass
near its stem sends the lights in the room

>> to curving.

With the naked eye, I would look for stars there—
out of necessity, as if I had a prayer,
as if I could drink them.

THE ASTRONOMER'S DREAM

The sky fell into the telescope—a tumble, then a dying
gasp. I sighed and scraped my toe on the observatory floor,

twisted the straps that held my glasses on, smiled.
The sky was a zero, an empty shell. When the data

stopped, the computer was a wreckage
of frozen points of light, confounded. The printer died

so I heard my breaths now loud as the whirr
of wheels that turned when I set the telescope

on a new and empty quadrant. *Freedom*, I thought,
my fingers at the soft focus. *Simple and quiet.*

All my life the stars were angry little sighs,
needle-pricks of breath. The sky coughed their light over me

so I'd grown accustomed and set my nights by them.
What more was there to say? I screwed the lens caps back

to bottle the starlight in. I shut the lamps
and closed the door behind me. The night was a wonder

of shadowless trees, a giant thrall—a wheeze from the dome
where the sky now was, then nothing at all.

STARS WHERE THEY AREN'T

They are not in the bloom in the grass, the slip of the hand
that threw seeds where the garden isn't. White flowers startle us,

haphazard on the lawn, but the stars are not in the curve of the petals.
Bees might slide their legs over the stamens' yellow brushes

and leave starry footprints on the windowsill, but they are not
in footprints and, no, not in star-struck eyes. When we sleep,

they are absent, though we see them in dreams.
Try to remember. What was their color? They are always changing

their minds. They are shifty as thieves and arrogant. Sting of the slice
from a spinning blade—we don't have the minds to measure them.

LAB NIGHTMARE

I dropped the microscope's slide; the room went numb.
Where did the blood on its surface go? I couldn't find it

in the thorns of glass beneath the counter, couldn't find it
as a stain on the floor or my plump gloved thumb.

The others turned and stared. I was tiny and dangerous
in my starched white coat, a contaminant for the lab

that heard the shards sing across the tiles. Had I released
the virus into the saferoom? Would we all be coughing

and paling soon? Bloom of bloodspot between the tile cracks,
drink for a terrible flower—they sealed the vacuum doors

and quarantined us in. So I am miserable and sorry now,
sulking in my chair in the corner of the lab. The air

has a retrovirus smell. The others pace the floor
in their white masks and goggles, check their blood

beneath the microscope's dumb eye, and curse me,
miserable me, half jointed in the thumb,

low-slung and guilty, breathing a dangerous pollen.

NARCISSISM

For this, still-fingered, I focused
my blue microscope until the fish's translucent scale
filled the fine lens's curved view.

What were the rays that shuddered to the scale's rim?
So onionlike, so much like my own iris's blacker lines
that tremble to my eye-white's inner edge?

Between the glass slide's surface and the lens's curve
it was as though another, finer, eye
stared up at me. I, who have never been

the subject of anything, was the world
into which it looked and what it saw came from myself.
I thought about my own eye's perfect brown.

When, finally, I lifted my head,
my lab, which once seemed ordered, white, bottle-lined,
caught the brilliant light

that passed through the room's high windows.

THE ARCHAEOLOGIST'S EVENING PRAYER

Were the artifacts hungry again?
The hooked bone harpoons, the men-of-clay
grinned and needily

ground their teeth. I hadn't eaten in three days
but spent each night with the static of a mosquito in my ears
and the distant sob of the African jackal.

The stone tools had gnawed at me—projectile points,
scraper and drill, core and saw until my fingers were eaten away.
I spent this morning in the yellow dust

brushing an ancient jaw clear of soil until,
from my knees, I looked down upon the strangest grin
I had ever seen: Seven teeth half animal and brown, too much chin bone,

a scattering of flint around it.
Constantly I found myself comparing the artifact
to the inappropriate: The teeth like a short string of shells. Or shining

as rows of dimes or pills. There was something of the key ring
in the fragment of the eyehole.
Then I imagined God descending from the yellow sky.

Did a light rain also come, tamping the clay back into place?
Giant-mouthed, He told me, *Touch your teeth. Chalk-like*
they will break from your mouth, crumble over your hands.

NEANDERTHAL

It's good enough, the finger bone
my brother uncovers at the site.
It's very white, a frosty white and cold.

Pale comma in the ground, insuck of breath,
pause, buried thought, the finger bone,
good enough—printless, but neanderthal.

All day he's labored at the trench
til now. He wipes his brow. The sun
was very white—is setting now.

He lifts the bone with the tip of his spade,
sets it in a cardboard box. He flags
the site—good enough to think about

as he rolls into dream that night,
the sleeping bag twisting at his ankles.
And cold and frosty white the stars

spin upward in the sky. *What will you do
with that box of bones?* they ask. *Are they
good enough to plant, those very white seeds?*

What color will the flowers be?

Two Muses Discuss Arrowheads

Two sloop-shouldered thin-legged young men beneath the Texaco sign
in Ohio, off state route 62, in the late afternoon, wearing blue jeans,
eating grapes:
                    Find them all-the-time, the first one says, splitting the green skin
between his thumb and index finger. *Got them sharp points, got them sides
cut through your hand*

                    *if you hold it too tight. Look like leaves, look like
no stone I seen around here. Shine in the sun, flinty, knob-ended, sharp,
sharp as busted up bits of skeet.*
                    The clear juice of grapes
trickles down his fingers, into the dirt. He holds up his hand. *Big as my hand,*
he says, *but longer, thinner.* His hand is beautiful, smooth and pale.

His hand has that glow of a car's headlamp coning the white mist in a dark road.
It is perfect, glistening, juice-slick. It seems to say, *watch me, watch me, watch me—
I could sever myself,*

                    skim the field-furrows, dig myself beneath the corn.
Around his feet, a scattering of discarded skins of white grapes, some dust-covered,
some pure and shimmering in the going sun

                    and the young man holds his hand up
a moment longer, flexes his long fingers into a point, *like that. Got me
a boxful.* His friend carves a long arc in the dirt

                    with his white shoe, shifts
where he sits on the curb's edge, nods, agrees. The sun goes down. The bright sign
glares. Like a thousand edgy little thoughts, the other thinks,

the arrowheads glow in their quiet places beneath the empty cornfields.

THE GOD OF CLUES

A fingerprint on the hammerhead, a bit of hair
in each tea cup,—I'm everywhere at once, diaphanous
or startling in my many colored suit.

I was overhead—the snow flakes sifted through me—
when you filled the wheelbarrow with garden sod
and shoveled the body in. I was laughing in my sleeve—

the earth tamped down, the flashlight crooked between
your shoulder and your chin. The street lights
were too bright, the moon too full, a telling bit

of soil clung to your boot tread. And there are worse things
still. Worse than this. The eyes of the dead
record their final vision. The cat on the porch stoop

heard it all, and now it's gone.
I filled the sky with crows. Your number's up.
It's going to rain, and soon the seed in the yard will sprout.

Four

. . . .

THIS WAS THE MODEL TO WHICH I HELD

This was the model to which I held:
a bee in its hole like a gasp
in my throat. Silence or dirge
as the petals unclasped,

dusted with blush at their folds.
This was the standard—I'd speak no word
when, after your long death, a thrill of bees
thrummed into the air, the chord

of their wings blaring flowers out.
This was my theory—I had no other—
the yard like a harlot, but you
still dead. Spring was a terror

of sensuous things—in my throat, a song
where a stinger hurt, where quiet belonged.

A MAN IN PEARLS

Who would say it's a man on the steps, a string of pearls
around the neck? Head bent into a corner,
pearls draped forward or knotted at the back

or fake—it's maybe strangled, but who can tell from so far?
It's maybe a red wilt around the neck, is perhaps wilted.
Is, we say, asleep.

It's probably, after all, not really a man.
Sometimes the streetlight baffles the crowd,
dropping a negligee over us all—and the snow, too,

like money or clipped blond hair.
Two witnesses huddle, mute, not too near
the steps, behind the police line. *Man, Pearls,*

the cop might write on his pad after taking a pulse,
though neither is certain. *The neck's crooked back,*
we murmur, in our knots. *Crooked* and *dead,* we say.

Or *Lipstick? Mascara?* But the lips are blue,
the eyes sunken in and dark. And the snow,
like cotton swabs, like talc, or lotion clots,

the snow spritzed or ashing over us
as the wind shifts and the cop snaps his notebook closed,
unfolds his phone, says, *No ID.* Says, *Toetag.*

Bag it. The cop says, *We got a dead man. Pearls.*

FOR THE DEAD

The fact that I still imagine your descent
as that of a white nightgown
falling through the laundry chute
between the walls of this empty house
is evidence enough for the primacy of the image
when the specific memory has gone.

For now, the beetles are waking in the twisted branches,
and now the traffic quickens its pulse
beneath the window. Is that your many-bladed heart
slicing up the grass on the neighbor's lawn?
I pull down the pouch beneath my eye
and lean into the bathroom mirror.

My iris' black lines
stretch through the blue like a stopped fan.

FOR THE DEAD

Are you smooth as the curve where the leaf stems out?
are you blush and clinging to the twig that fell
where the mailbox sprouts from its weed thicket?
no, no—you are underexposed, a photo snapped
with the sun too low and subtle over the grass.
Oh, inscrutable as light in the too-wide yard—I'll wait
at the screen door, fingers curved to the metalwork.

And when the sun ticks so heavy over the house
that the shingles fight their nails to curl,
and the bees' nest drones and sways above the door,
how can I not expect a sign or unclick the latch?
The bees are heat-swelled and dangerous, dripping
from the gutter, all trickery and words that sound
like yours—*Love, my season of too much*
light, of heat on twigs where the wind has felled them,
I was almost dead when the great moon cut the trees.
I was gone when the dust moths shed their wings.

FOR THE DEAD

A gray wind gutters the fireflies
to the edge of the yard where tomatoes
hang like droop-headed lanterns,

wired and sweet. Engineered
to skitter, many legged and cased in husks—
each firefly is the sum of its engineering,

a flare I can't put my finger on. When I was young
I loved them for this reason: the tension
of wings as they arced over, their veins

essential as wires and invisible, the mystery
of their spark. Each mechanical thing is more intricate
than the dead, who hide in our gardens

and finger our plants, more tangible than God
who, when he breathes, clears the yard of complications.

FOR THE DEAD: ADORATION

I died, so they laid me in a room pierced by street lamps.
Go on, go on I said to the cutting of tires on the rain-slick
street. *Go on*
          to the click on black windows, to the indefatigable
poise of friends.

*

A multitude of wrong ways to see death:
a closing in the eyes,
          a final heave of the breath—a crowd,
wet-in-the-eyes, carrying the gone, after dark,
to the edge of the city. A wailing.

*

The dead are not sad portraits in oils. The mourning
can't blot their cheeks
          with thumbprints.

The dead can't be kept or held,
          can't be carried off, can't turn
in their bedclothes.
          My clothes were painted to my skin.
I had no weight.

*

It is not that God doesn't speak when the dying
stop, but that he can't be found in the room:
          A quiet breath
in every tree-top, a stirring below the window—

*

So the city woke as a newborn, with a twitch and a wail.
The sun came up like a long cry.
          I counted back the seconds
as the sky grayed and the first doors slammed.
There and there I said.
          Five four three—the street lamps died
as the sun warmed the breaths of the waking.

FOR THE DEAD: A CLEARER SONG

I am trying to sing a clearer song, don't go.
                                But the wind is a crook,
it steals my words away. And the snow comes down like laundry
through the chute, comes down like comets trailing sheets of gas,
like spiders on their silver strings.
                                The sun—strung down

*

hours ago, and on the bed with the last gas lamps on dim,
I felt my body leave. The loved ones gathered around—
sang songs into a cold draft,
                                wrung their kerchiefs, crossed
my fingers and prayed for a final gasp
                                of day, the last twitch
in the thick muscle at my shoulder blade. Lord, lord,

*

a divinity was lost in the room.
                                It is so easy to sing a perfect dirge
for another, but I can't praise you properly, can't sing my gratitude
in notes. I spill myself clumsily, like snows under the door,
                                with the wind.

*

Won't someone come forward and take over this song?
Won't a person of authority?
                                Won't you, thin-fingered
divinity, with all your grace and snow?

LETTER OF CONSOLATION

The dead are inaccessible
                          as a blackened window
and the untranslatable night where the glass ends

Our palms cup the pane
                          or our palms   hot buds in our laps.

The reflection of stars rolls over the windows
                                      runs pointy fingers
over the glass
                 fogs the glass with each hot breath.

Spring nights we are always talking about asters
                                      their tongues move too slowly
they trouble the soil   part the garden where you threw the seeds
do not trust a living thing
                          that is this slow to speech.

The hush-hearted river behind the house
                                      talks all night
the trees could drop their leaves over it   could scatter it with twigs
do not trust it.

I had too much wine at dinner   it dogged my steps   filled my mouth
with flowers
                 you can never talk to the dead again I said
before I had time to regret.

Sometimes wine makes a petal of my tongue
                          sweet words

                                      a gloom and sting.
you will never you will never

Leaved things grow out of the vanished

                                               vine-like and startling

from the mouths of the taken
       the drawn-away stars.

BLUE PITCHER, EMPTY AND FULL

You will use it for the flowers the others bring because he is dead.

Or you will use it for dark blue light, the arc of it when, the next evening, the
    sun cries over the house and sends all the windows to the floor.

A trill of orchids wilts over the rim. You will use them for perspective. The petals
    fall when you're asleep like petals in dreams, dying to stop.

You will use them for silence, when the room is a rumble of passing trains and
    his picture rattles over the end tables.

"You'll use it for flowers," I said the other day, placing the blue pitcher on the
    windowsill, turning it so it balanced there. The windows were cold to
    the touch because it was almost winter and the wind blew from the
    lake.

When the relatives left, the house was a hush. The tracks bent into the woods
    along the lake, the pitcher looking out the window like a great
    blue eye.

I know you are reading this in the fragility of evening, when the rain comes in
    from the lake and simmers over the house.

I know you are reading in the half light, your fingers covered with flour, the oven
    on and a silence from the kitchen where the bread is baking.

The house juts over the lake on spindles. The pitcher paints a blue arc on the
    floor. There is no one upstairs.

The Last of the Storm Windows

Once, at the end of winter, some years back, my face against
the screen to breathe the new air that was not, after all, so cold,
and the bees singing *give me, give me, give me* to the pinks

that were just poking through the loam in my mother's garden,
and the apple blossoms like wantons all lipsticked up
at the tips of their little green buds—once,

and this was years ago, when, after a particularly cold winter
in the small town in Missouri where I have lived all my life,
the lawn was a squabble of wanting things, was blush and trilling,

the grass bent like courtesans and the mailbox showering
its white flowers all over the drive—then, for a moment,
I left my body. I left my body but, in the blink of it, looked down

at my rigid self bent over the screen, the storm window
half removed, a litter of paint chips at my knees. I was thick-limbed,
the doll a boy props on the sill then, with a stick, knocks

to its ground. Some day, I knew, my heart would stop in its package.
My mouth would close, my tongue thick over. I was a greedy thing.
I thought a bird once made her nest in the back of my throat.

There, where I had always ached to eat or speak,
I felt the hungry rustle of a dozen tiny beaks.

WHAT THE PAYMASTER SAID

Instead of a paycheck, the company offered me kind thoughts. *We'll give you three*, the paymaster said, *one for your diligence and two for your beautiful wife.* No, no. I did not want their kind thoughts. I'd had enough of them.

If not that, the paymaster said, *then what about apples? They are delicious apples, fresh from Wisconsin, and sweet. Under every one, the fruitpicker has held his palm, has wobbled each apple until it fell ripely into his hand of its own accord. Three bushels.* But I did not want their apples. I wanted what was mine.

We must learn not to be selfish in difficult times, the paymaster said, *but you type quite well. You type superbly, your fingers flashing across the keyboard like beautiful blades of tall grass when the wind blows from the distant mountains. I will give you cigarettes for your typing, or I will give you bombs.*

The bombs are quite nice. They fall from airplanes which you will rent by the hour. The company will lease you an airplane at a discounted rate, but the bombs will be yours to keep. You have such a pleasant manner, we can't afford to lose you. So I make this fine offer. I shook my head. I didn't want cigarettes or bombs. I have many mouths to feed, and my wife would not be happy if I brought home only bombs.

The paymaster sighed and adjusted his coat so the gold buttons winked in the office lights. *You are ungrateful*, he told me, *but I will offer you one more thing. Instead of a paycheck, I will give you coffins. The grain is as fine as a dragonfly's wing. Coffins for your entire family—all at the company's generous expense.*

THE LOVED ONES

—Marguerite Duras, *The War*

I decided to leave a space in which the din of the war might be remembered.

I measured it out, fifteen feet by thirty, so that it would conform to my front lawn.

You say that a place I can measure in blades of grass is not enough?
I tell you we are talking about families who have lost loved ones.

Fifteen by thirty will suffice. There is always a house at a lawn's fore.
Beyond this, it is traversed each day by drying leaves and cats.

And what of that other country, across the black sea?

There, they sit at outdoor café tables.
They fill the glasses again and again with a mixture of carbonated water and wine.
Sometimes there is a tolling of a bell

at which point they rise and wander down the street.

Do they walk aimlessly? Their cities are not laid out like our own.
Their streets are narrow and turn suddenly.

THE LIVING

This is not about my life. I was reading the menu,
I was part of a *Résistance*, someone dropped a glass of wine.
The singing of glass was everywhere
and the clear leaves were all over the bar.
Sleep, sleep, somebody said

but it was part of a conversation I couldn't get the gist of.
Did I know the lines at Arles had fallen?
Had I heard about the swamps outside St. Pierre?
Each day, I read the lists in the newspaper

and his name was never among them.
There are reports that our retreating soldiers
saw red leaves shuffling strangely in the winds
until angels rose through the highest branches
and saved them with their wings.

The man who spilled his drink was singing now.
He raised his broken glass to the lights.
In the jagged stem was the tiniest red stone of wine,
which he swallowed. The crowd applauded.

Every day, more names.
We all pretend to believe the story about angels.
I think the world takes place on the surface of a brilliant red leaf.
When the wind blows and the tree shakes,
things fall closer to that leaf's black veins.

KINDS OF SLEEP

There is the sleep of the plastic soldier and it is olive green and terrible on the windowsill where the sun speckles the dust so, like mortar, it hangs in the air

and there is the sleep of the window, which is clear and cool to the touch.

I love the dream of the yard beyond the window, which is at peace, how the sun swags over the trees like a little gold watch suspended from a chain, the hypnotist saying, *sleep, now. I will count to three.*

My daughter lines plastic soldiers on the windowsill. This is a serious game, picking one soldier after another from a coffee can.

I have never been to war, though I often dream about a battle in Super8, where extras pose on a ridge while the night air trills and the mortar falls like a hot glass net.

Always, the mind goes back to a story about angels rising from the trees. First there was a fluttering in the leaves above the war, then they spread their golden wings

over the bodies of the retreating. This is the myth, dreamed in grainy black & white, the camera shaking while the soldiers slipped on the ice,

slipped and fell but—gratefully, gratefully—made it over the hill and back to their tents where the director yelled *cut* and the extras smiled and collected their checks.

I fear most the sleeps of the dead, strewn like spent cartridges where the guns eject them.

FOR THE UNFORTUNATES

Forgive me, insomniacs. I dozed off. I fell into a dream. I slipped, here at the kitchen counter, with the apples, looking over the lawn.

And you, the wounded. Will you forgive me? I cut my finger on this paring knife. It stains the sink, but not so badly. I bit my lip to keep from crying and now the water washes the basin clean.

You, who haven't room in your heads for a new thought: I live in a windmill. All day long, the blades swing round, the hundred cogs above the roof clicking away like excellent ideas. Forgive me. My ears are full of cotton, but it does no good.

Wood bugs in my walls, wasps in my bread box—they aren't laughing at you, who have no feeling in your thumbs, the numb at heart. Their mouths are full of woodchips, their eyes blind with paint.

Won't you all be kind? I have so many gentle thoughts. Forgive me, unfortunates: there is a little knife in my hand.

THE END OF THE CITY

Now only the dying and as the sky closes its shutter I say
I walked with them I talked with them I speak their names again
and count them on my fingers I count back on my fingers.

And now the trees drop their leaves into the avenue
and the cars have stopped so the leaves billet the windshields.
Now the sun is beautiful as a tear rolling down the sky.

When the Romans came Carthage dropped through the trees
and when the Visigoths came Rome fell like an old coin
and with the plague Antioch tripped in its boots.

Cities fall and sometimes like old men rise on their joints
so as my city stumbled I was on the phone saying
Thank you for calling please ring me up again to the dead air

my words failing and my hands growing cold.
And as the dying turned in their beds I was saying
Lord lord raise them up and keep their feet from sliding

but from the west where the wind comes *dead air*
and from above where the street lamps nod on their posts *no light*.
I do not remember a war I do not remember a pestilence

I did not provoke the avenues into such a silence.

TROMPE L'OEIL

The dead are as an echo resounding off a wall
on which someone has painted the shapes of stars.

My mittens unravel. The long strands
flutter against my coat sleeves. I put my fingers in my mouth
where they will be warm. In the air again, the weave stiffens,

shells over. Snow falls as stars or, cast in a deceiving light, as dying
embers. Shadows thrown by street lamps so each black footprint
appears larger than it ought to be, the low crying

of wind, an echo thereof, the evening slowing, stopping—
does the mind tick to a close like this?

—————————

In January of 1610, cast adrift by a mutinous crew, Henry Hudson
and his young son were never seen again, or

it is 1912 and Xavier Mertz slips into a crevice, legs twisted
behind him. He calls and calls, but the rope isn't long enough.
Please don't ask me to explain—It is 1820

and the British load their lifeboats
with candlesticks and china, lash them with ropes, and set out,
dragging them across the Canadian tundra.

It is any year at all. The landscapes thicken, crust over,
all the people clicking forward, their minds

—————————

slowly unticking. I have seen from below the domes of cathedrals
designed to convince us that they are not there

at all. Someone painted them a perfect bottle blue,
traced over them with the outlines of stars which, later,
he gilded—so even in the weakest candlelight

they shone as though they were real. I stood, head tilted,
and looked into an unmoving sky. I whispered my name,
and heard the echo come back to me.